Hiraeth

Arnabi Mallick

BookLeaf
Publishing

India | USA | UK

Made with ❤ on the BookLeaf Publishing Platform

www.bookleafpub.in

www.bookleafpub.com

Dedication

To Sakshi and my little sisters, Diya and Duti

Preface

Hiraeth: a Welsh word with no direct English translation —a homesickness for a place that no longer exists or perhaps never was; a profound longing for home, tinged with grief for something lost yet still remembered in the marrow of one's bones.

In these pages, I have attempted to map the contours of this exquisite ache. The poems collected here explore the liminal spaces between belonging and displacement, between memory and imagination, between what was and what might have been. They are meditations on absence that somehow become a presence of their own.

Each verse emerged from that peculiar intersection where personal history meets universal human experience—that shared understanding that we are all, in some measure, reaching for something just beyond our grasp. These words found me in quiet moments, in fragments of dreams, in echoes of conversations, in the silences between heartbeats.

I offer these poems not as resolutions but as companions for your journey through the landscapes of remembrance and yearning. May they resonate with your own experience of *hiraeth*, that beautiful, necessary ache that reminds us we are human.

Acknowledgements

I owe a debt of gratitude to PD, whose gentle nudges and occasional habit of giving me small existential crises pushed me to both begin and complete this journey. To Sakshi, my unwavering best friend—your steadfast support has been my sanctuary through every doubt and celebration. To Baba, for believing in me. I'm eternally grateful to Srujana, whose artistic vision brought this book to life through its cover and whose encouragement sustained me throughout the process. And to Manoswita, who patiently weathered my self-doubt —your patience has been an invaluable gift. This book exists because each of you, in your own way, helped me believe it could.

1. Sisyphus and the fly

Why not weep for Satan?
Why must you kill a fly but not a butterfly?
Why must Romeo and Juliet be together?
And why did Sisyphus continue to roll the boulder up
the hill?

Perhaps because someone had to be the fallen angel,
So that others could feel a semblance of power.
It's permissible to kill a fly,
for beauty often shapes empathy.
And who can resist a love story?
So what if Juliet could have forged a life of her own?

For Sisyphus, he was just stuck in the cycle of futility
But could he just get under the boulder
When it rolled down the hill just before reaching the top,
Just when Sisyphus had a miniscule fragment of hope
That he might have just made it.
And he kept doing it again and again and again

Wouldn't he be better off dead?
Oh but that's no way to end it, is it?

You must suffer because it's beautiful
Or else what's the difference between Sisyphus and a fly?

2. The two syllables

I read a quote that said
"Your smile was a metaphor
I have been trying to write for years"
I thought about you when I read this.

"He wouldn't think of you when he reads this," the voice echoed,
Perhaps it was right—you wouldn't.
I deceive myself into believing
I'm okay with that.

Only to fill my pages with the remnants of you.
I haven't transcended above my fragile affections
Neither have I learnt to silence them.

They scream at my fears
But I hear all of them in two syllables,
The syllables turn into a sweet symphony
Of the sun set sky,
The two syllables of Oranges, Reds, pinks, and purples,
Turn into a dark blue of the ocean at night.

3. The moth and the girl

The moth flew through the room
The room housed the girl
Sitting on her bed,
Words blew through the smoke through her lips
The solitary moth flew through the smoke twirls.
The tubelight was brightly lit,
The windows were open
But the moth refused to leave.
The hands were tired, so were the legs.
The moth was still flying in circles.
The girl lay down on the bed,
Something red traced her palms down her wrists,
The month, tired, fatigued fell down on the bed,
The tubelight now started flickering.

4. Mirror and the Stranger

I gaze upon a stranger's eyes,
Reflected back from the glass mirror.

I ask, "Mirror Mirror who is this person?"
The mirror responds, "I don't see anyone"
I ask again, "What do you see then?"
"I see a half burnt cigarette,
I see trembling hands,
Eyes wet with guilt of the past
And I see unrequited attachments."

"Why don't you see me?", I exasperated.
"Because you are lost in an abyss,
Abyss of broken things,
Broken furniture,
Broken glass
Torn pages,
Broken relations,
Screams,
Broken home."

"Where am I here?", I cry.
"You are not,

You exist in the existence of all things broken and torn,
You exist in the invisibility of your kin
You are not here but you beg to be
For nobody sees your scars, so you keep wounding
yourself
I see a beggar".

5. Turning 14

I remember the gentle sea breeze
And the salty humidity.
I remember your indifference
The dissociation and the deception.

I was 14, I turned 14 that day,
But I wish my existence was full and void,
Void like your eyes for me Mother
What had I so done to receive no love?
Love that is said to soothe
Love that melts the rocks.

What had I done to sharpen your heart so finely
That it chopped away my innocence that day.
I didn't see roses, but burning bushes of flowers
That day.
I didn't see love, I saw something die inside you and me.

6. All Red

All the blood,
this blood gets absorbed in the soil floor.
The dust on the bed clings to my hair,
And the heat burns my skin.

The footsteps keep getting louder
Until it reaches the Damsel
I was not in distress or pain
It was like ice rubbing on the skin
Again and Again
The same place, same space.

While I watched the blood drip,
The night-blooming jasmines turned red,
It was all just red.

7. Love has never been home

Love has never been kind
Love has been the hot light bulb to an insect
It has been the ash in a wood fire
It's the residue of stickers on cutlery.

Love has been a stranger on the metro,
An indifferent route to a known address,
A blow of wind on a cold morning.
A heap of roughly torn pages.

Love, is not familiar with warmth,
But the cold of rubbing ice,
The accidental wounds across the body,
The incidental scratches.

Love has never been home
It has been to apartments,
Parks and places,
Forests and mazes.

Just not home,
just not yet,
just not never.

I breathe into disappointment,
A known disappointment,
An accepted one.

I breathe into the ruins of words,
Words turned to ashes
And muted voices.

If death replaces me
I would exist in whispers.
Whispers of all things waiting,
All things incomplete,
All things untouched,
All things rotting,
All things dead.

8. Grief

I never conversed with grief,
I argued with it.
For it never gave me enough time,
Enough time to meet
Enough time to share a chocolate cake with coffee
To listen to recitations of elegant poetry
To say goodbyes.
I postponed grief and it never left me.

9. Poetry and its selfishness

People are poetry.
The sheer existence of one,
And the mundanity of this existence from
One sunrise to another,
Before they burn down to dust
Or dry down to their bones.

The art of breathing,
Thoughts that inhale and exhale out
Effortlessly, like it was almost never there
The impermanence of it.

The broken figments of imagination
Diving from one curve to another
Stuck in a labyrinth.

People say the heart breaks
But does it really?
Or is it the utter shock of discomfort?
Isn't it the fear of finding new ways to live life
Isn't it the uncanny that we fear when something is
lost?
Isn't it all just selfish?
Isn't poetry nothing but defending this selfishness?

10. The Upstairs room

The upstairs room would fill up with heat,
The burning afternoon sun rays would
Drill holes in my skin,
While I lay in bed, quiet, calm, and patient.
Patient to leave the room.

When the fingers would stop lingering over me.
Calm like a sleeping puppy
Something kept feeling heavy in the room.
Quiet so that the hands won't hurt.

The stairs to the upstairs room were rather dark
But the room felt darker
The footsteps would get louder
No two visits to the room were the same
But every time, I was quiet, calm and patient.

11. Some days

And on some days,
Days like these,
I wish I were dead.

Only a passive audience to everything that's around
And not a recipient of it.
I wish I were not here
I wish I were nowhere.

Just a distant memory
Or a reverie of someone far away in the woods
Who is as distant from everything
As I am from myself.

12. Tombstone

I drew the curtains
And stopped the rays of the setting sun
From stabbing itself into the four walls
Of my impending gloom.
On days like these
I wish I were dead
Only a passive audience to everything that's around
And not a recipient of it
I wish I was not here
I wish I was no where
Just a distant memory
A reverie of someone far away in the woods
Who is as distant from everything
As I am from myself.

The evening sky is calm and quiet
I sit and scribble in my exuberant fatigue
The mundanity of this existence from
One sunrise to another,
Before it burns down to dust
Or dries down to its bones.
The art of breathing,
Thoughts that inhale and exhale out
Effortlessly, like it was almost never there

The impermanence of it
The broken figments of imagination
Diving from one curve to another
Stuck in a labyrinth.

The night air tears me apart
Chokes me to my lungs
The air is cold and so is the water
I drown my skin in the sheer coldness
My body wants to resist
My hands trying to hold on to the air
My feet trying to find a land
And then at midnight,
I am calm
I am colder than the air or the water
Quieter than the dawn.
Still, like the stones in the cemetery.

13. Hiraeth

I see you in my broken dreams
With my little childhood
And a heavy book.
You read out a poem,
But it wasn't the same,
The same one that summons tears
The one that breaks my smile.
I request you to read it,
You do. I cry.
This is a distant reverie.

All this love and anger I have stored for you mother,
Will you hold me while I hold onto those?
I am angry with you because you ask me to not cry
But never did you wipe my tears
I am angry because I have so much love for you
Yet I don't know how to hold your hand
I am angry with you because there is so much love in me
for you
That it chokes me and you don't come to save me
Instead you enjoy the show.
The show of my longing for you.

14. Lilies and Poison ivy

I think life likes to add paradoxes here and there.
Like she and I,
We send each other poems that talk about love,
Different kinds of love,
The one that wasn't reciprocated
The one that consumes you
The one that was lost and never found
But I found it in him
And she did too.

Except I lost it, again
And she got it anew.
Whatever the atoms in our bodies reach for,
Look for, understand and yearn for,
Her's and mine are the same.
Except she gets to melt in his little embraces
My abstracts just boomerang back to me.

In the empty room or on the isolated roof.
The air around me condenses on my bare skin
And I keep breathing even when she is too close to him
She feels like being surrounded by lilies
And I like being trapped by poison ivy.

Just not poisonous enough,
But enough to infect me from within.

15. Love and other drugs

Love's incompleteness blooms in silent spaces.
The pain of losing it all.
Not having it all.
The sheer ache it causes,
The numbing ache.
The distance,
The distanced closeness.
The yearning,
The insufferable yearning.
The numbness,
The indifferent numbness.
The agony of it all.
There's a hint of beauty in it
The ability to love something unachievable,
Something that cannot be one's own.
The utter loveliness of the deadly torment,
How we love to love and pain to let it go
But love anyway.

16. A poet without poetry

Sometimes there is no poetry in the poet
And that is how they best understand the yearning for
the love that was lost
The absence of something unfathomable
But the existence with the pain of it's absence.

A poet without poetry,
A love without a lover
It's so incomplete that it's almost unreal,
Until you read the poet's eyes,
Until you see the broken lines in the half torn pages.

That's when the irony settles.
You can be robbed of what was meant for you
And still admire it,
Still have it in some metaphysical way
In the form of a cosmic synergy of what you wish and
what you have.

17. I wait for you to forget me.

On one slow day I see you lingering in your room
Your perfectly sculpted hands tie me to you
I feel at peace when my skin gets to feel the warmth of
yours,
When I can smell your smell and recognize it at once.

We stay like this, but only for a snippet.
And then days go by when I wait for you to yearn for me
again
To want to tell me that there's too much light on the
other side of the curtain.
I wait till you forget me and want to remember me again.
I wait for you to forget me.

18. Fall in Love

Like they say, you "fall" in love
You really do, but how do you get up?
How do I get up?
I saw you getting up and walking into an oblivion,
Assimilating with the bright sunrays at the end of the
tunnel,
It must be autumn there,
I see you have let go of your shawl
And I am here trying to crawl but just tripping again and
again
In the cold dry soil,
Falling over and over again
Like they say, you fall in love.

19. Red Canvas

Every bit of her is dripping off her body,
Her bones, slowly turning into something red, like blood.
Different shades of red
There are shadows and depths,
And in those depths are eyes
Eyes lingering around,
Eyes she doesn't want on her
Or on the little girl beside her.
Some hands crawl out of these shadows
Not in the light, not for it will burn
But, for it will shame not the hands but the legs.
So she takes a brush and paints every canvas red,
Until there is no more, no one.

20. How does death arrive?

How does death arrive?
I have been wondering
For too long now
And waiting for it for quite some time.

When pain infects you like death
But death doesn't address you
It makes you tired,
The elysian way of life,
Is not something you want anymore,
It's just death, not a pause, a stop.

Pain felt like death in little capsules
But especially when you said what you said
It had to be this way
The only way
But why this way is what I still can't quite comprehend,
Until now.

That felt like death piercing into me
Leaving me to bleed,
Slowly, just enough each day.
Let the old blood dry,
And the fresh blood of the day

Adds dimension of blacks and reds
And refusing to free me from it.
Death laughed at me and left me.

21. Curse

One life,
Two places to be,
But you want to be in three.
Divisions of heart,
Walls of stone
Too opaque to let me in,
Too transparent to sin.

All this trouble will be worth it,
Only if you don't realize what you did
Only if you forget the summer we played,
The balloons we slayed.

The smiles for which I would kill
Those memories feel so still
The pride that I took
The trust that I put
The love I couldn't let go
It was a curse that I didn't know.

www.ingramcontent.com/pod-product-compliance
Lightning Source LLC
LaVergne TN
LVHW021807210726
843510LV00018B/1672